Davy
Crockett

A Buddy Book
by
Christy DeVillier

ABDO
Publishing Company

VISIT US AT

www.abdopub.com

Published by ABDO Publishing Company, 4940 Viking Drive, Suite 622, Edina, Minnesota 55435. Copyright © 2004 by Abdo Consulting Group, Inc. International copyrights reserved in all countries. No part of this book may be reproduced in any form without written permission from the publisher.

Printed in the United States.

Edited by: Michael P. Goecke
Contributing Editor: Matt Ray
Image Research: Deborah Coldiron
Graphic Design: Jane Halbert
Cover Photograph: Library of Congress
Interior Photographs/Illustrations: Hulton Archives, Library of Congress, North Wind, Photodisc, PhotoSpin

Library of Congress Cataloging-in-Publication Data

Devillier, Christy, 1971-
    Davy Crockett / Christy Devillier.
        v. cm. — (First biographies)
    Includes index.
    Contents: Who is Davy Crockett?—Growing up—Frontier life—Creek War—Lawmaker—Fighting for Texas—American hero.
    ISBN 1-59197-512-3
    1. Crockett, Davy, 1786-1836—Juvenile literature. 2. Pioneers—Tennessee—Biography—Juvenile literature. 3. Frontier and pioneer life—Tennessee—Juvenile literature. 4. Tennessee—Biography—Juvenile literature. 5. Legislators—United States—Biography—Juvenile literature. 6. United States. Congress. House—Biography—Juvenile literature. 7. Alamo (San Antonio, Tex.)—Siege, 1836—Juvenile literature. [1. Crockett, Davy, 1786-1836. 2. Pioneers. 3. Legislators. 4. Alamo (San Antonio, Tex.)—Siege, 1836.] I. Title.

F436.C95D48 2004
976.8'04'092—dc21
[B]
                                                                2003052263

Table Of Contents

Who Is Davy Crockett?

   Davy Crockett was a hero of the Wild West. He lived on the American frontier about 200 years ago.

   Davy Crockett was a skilled hunter, lawmaker, and storyteller. He was also a soldier. Davy Crockett fought in the famous Texas battle at the Alamo.

Davy Crockett is a hero of the American frontier.

Growing Up

Davy Crockett was born on August 17, 1786. He grew up in Tennessee. He moved with his family to Jefferson County in 1796.

Davy started school when he was about 13 years old. One day, he got in a fight with a classmate. Davy did not return to school.

United States of America

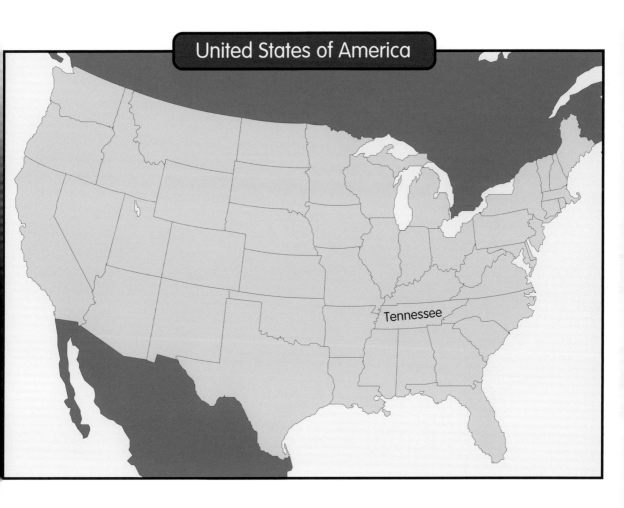

Tennessee

Davy's father was angry when he learned Davy skipped school. So, Davy ran away from home. He worked for other men. Davy farmed and drove cattle. He helped on wagon trains, too.

After about two years, Davy went home. His family was very happy to see him.

Davy Crockett's first home was a log cabin.

Frontier Life

Davy Crockett married Mary Finley on August 12, 1806. Mary's nickname was Polly. Davy and Polly lived on a farm in Tennessee. They had three children.

Davy and his family moved to Franklin County, Tennessee, in 1813. Davy wanted to live on the Tennessee frontier. They settled in a log cabin on Bean's Creek.

Davy Crockett hunted bears and other animals.

Davy enjoyed living on the wild frontier. Like other settlers, he often hunted animals for food. Davy hunted deer, bears, and other animals.

Davy was a skilled hunter. He had a rifle he called Betsy. Davy said he once shot 100 bears in one season. He may have killed a 600-pound (272-kg) bear, too.

Davy Crockett was a skilled hunter.

Creek War

In the 1800s, settlers moved farther and farther west. They often lived near American Indians. Sometimes, settlers and the American Indians did not get along. Fights broke out.

Fights between settlers and the American Indians were common on the frontier.

In 1813, Creek Indians attacked settlers at Fort Mims. Many settlers died. This was the beginning of the Creek War.

Davy Crockett was a scout in the Creek War. He served under General Andrew Jackson.

The Creek War ended in 1814. One year later, Davy Crockett's wife, Polly, died.

A Creek Indian attack on Fort Mims started the Creek War.

Lawmaker

Over time, Davy got to know his neighbor, Elizabeth Patton. In 1816, Davy married Elizabeth. They moved to Lawrence County, Tennessee.

A wedding in the 1800s.

Lawrence County did not have a government. Davy Crockett became the county judge. The people thought his rulings were fair.

In 1821, Davy ran for a state office. He wanted to become a Tennessee lawmaker. Telling funny stories helped him win many votes. Davy was a Tennessee lawmaker for four years.

Davy's goal was helping poor Tennessee settlers. The settlers trusted Davy. He understood their problems.

In 1827, Davy became a U.S. Representative for Tennessee. He tried to pass laws that would help poor farmers. Davy served six years in the U.S. Congress.

The U.S. Congress meets at the Capitol building in Washington, D.C.

Fighting For Texas

In 1835, Davy Crockett decided to move to Texas. Back then, Mexico ruled Texas.

Many settlers from America lived in Texas. These Texans were tired of Mexican rule. Texans wanted independence from Mexico.

In 1836, Davy Crockett joined the Tennessee Mountain Volunteers. The volunteers vowed to help Texans fight for independence. They met with Colonel William B. Travis in San Antonio, Texas.

Colonel Travis knew a Mexican army was on their way. He wanted to defend San Antonio. So, he led Davy and the other Texans into a fort. This fort was the Alamo.

General Antonio López de Santa Anna was the leader of the Mexican army. They began attacking the Alamo on February 23, 1836. They set up cannons and fired at the fort.

The Alamo still stands today.

The Texans shot at the Mexican soldiers with Kentucky long rifles. They held back General Santa Anna's army for about two weeks.

On March 6, 1836, the Mexican army broke into the Alamo. All the Texans died defending the Alamo. Davy Crockett died there, too.

Santa Anna's army won the battle at the Alamo.

American Hero

Davy Crockett was a frontier hero even before he died at the Alamo. People read tall tales about him in the Davy Crockett almanacs. People loved hearing Davy's famous saying: Be always sure you are right, then go ahead.

Many Americans have not forgotten Davy Crockett. There are songs and plays about him. There are television shows and movies about Davy's life, too.

Davy Crockett is a hero for many Americans today. His exciting life is an important part of American history.

Important Dates

August 17, 1786 Davy Crockett is born.

1796 Davy and his family move to Jefferson County, TN.

1806 Davy marries Mary Finley.

1813 Davy joins the United States Army as a scout. He fights in the Creek War.

1815 Mary Finley dies.

1816 Davy marries Elizabeth Patton.

1821–1824 Davy serves as a Tennessee lawmaker.

1827 Davy is voted into the United States House of Representatives.

1835 Davy begins his move to Texas.

March 6, 1836 Davy Crockett dies defending the Alamo.

Important Words

almanac a book printed each year with information on many subjects.

fort a building with four walls to protect against enemies.

frontier wild land that has not been settled.

independence freedom.

tall tales stories that make someone or something seem greater or bigger.

Web Sites

To learn more about Davy Crockett, visit ABDO Publishing Company on the World Wide Web at www.abdopub.com. Web sites about Davy Crockett are featured on our Book Links page. These links are routinely monitored and updated to provide the most current information available.

Index